Talk for Maths

Jenny Penfold

CONTENTS

How to use this resource — 2

Teacher's notes and photocopymasters — 4

Content focus and classroom techniques — 64

INTRODUCTION

Mind's Eye Talk for Maths encourages children to think about mathematics and to explore ideas using images as a starting point for mathematical discussion.

The National Strategies emphasise that:
- seeing mathematics through models and images supports learning
- talking mathematics clarifies and refines thinking.

It is widely accepted that speaking and listening plays a vital role in the development of understanding in all subjects including mathematics:

Language is an integral part of most learning and oral language in particular has a key role in classroom teaching and learning ... in their daily lives, children use speaking and listening to solve problems, speculate, make decisions and reflect on what is important.

(Speaking, Listening and Learning Handbook, DfES 0626-2003 G)

Speaking and listening is one of the most important aspects of this book. Each of the 30 images on the CD-ROM can be used as a starting point for mathematics and also for the development of these skills. Children are encouraged to engage in whole-class discussion and also to work in different types of groupings. They are expected to use mathematical vocabulary and to share and explain their methods, solutions, choices, decisions and reasoning. Reasoning and communicating are key aspects of the 'using and applying mathematics' strand of the *Primary Framework for mathematics* (2006).

Children are encouraged to participate in productive talk which involves:
- making suggestions or introducing new ideas
- supporting other people's suggestions
- challenging ideas
- reasoning or justifying
- asking questions
- summarising
- analysing and evaluating.

Paired and group work can facilitate the development of these skills. This book offers effective ways in which these can be implemented.

- **Envoy.** These activities begin in groups and then one child – the envoy – visits one or more groups to share and compare information, solutions and results. On returning to the original group, all information gathered by the envoy and from visiting envoys is shared and compared.
- **Home group of mixed ability children.** Lower attaining children often understand and learn better from other children's explanations. They can be encouraged and their expectations raised when working with more confident children. Higher attaining children who are reluctant talkers have opportunities to explain their thinking in clear ways, in a non-threatening setting. Children consolidate their thinking by explaining to others.
- **Hot seating.** The class asks questions of someone who sits in the 'hot seat'.
- **Listening triangles.** Children work in groups of three. They take turns to speak and listen before reporting to the large group. Sometimes a listener is assigned while the other two children discuss.
- **Rainbowing.** Each member of a group is given a colour. Children work in this group initially. Later they form new groups by joining other children allocated the same colour. They compare findings in their new groups.
- **Snowballing.** Children have a short while to think individually about questions posed. They share their ideas with a partner and then together with another pair.
- **Talk partners.** Pairs take turns to speak and listen to each other. It is useful to keep the same pairings for a period to help children gain confidence.
- **Think, pair, share.** Similar to 'snowballing' but, instead of sharing with another pair, each pair shares with the class.

HOW TO USE *MIND'S EYE TALK FOR MATHS*

1. Select a *Talk for Maths* activity that fits with your teaching. Read through the teacher's notes and check the resources needed.
2. Project the image onto a screen or interactive whiteboard to capture children's interest.
3. Ask children for an initial response to what they see and introduce the background information detailed in the introduction as appropriate.
4. Explore the image further with children using the suggested discussion points to develop and consolidate topic-related vocabulary through talk.
5. Use the activity suggestions and organise children into suitable pairs or groups. Children will need to discuss ideas with their partner or group and explain their reasoning to their partner or others in the group.
6. Use the 'challenge' and photocopymasters for independent problem solving either as a lesson follow-up or for homework.
7. The Assessment for Learning (AfL) question at the end of each session focuses on a key area of mathematics from the lesson. Use this to assess children and inform further teaching.

ACTIVITIES

To help organise your teaching, this table maps each activity to the planning blocks and units of the *Primary Framework*.

Block	Unit 1	Unit 2	Unit 3
A Counting, partitioning and calculating	Snowmen p4 Count away p6	In my home p8 Making numbers p10	Car numbers p12 Animal sums p14
B Securing number facts, understanding shape	Triangles and squares p16 Dominoes p18	Money box p20 Would you rather? p22 Patterns p24	Airbrick patterns p26 Cupcakes p28 Shapes and patterns p30
C Handling data and measures	Sorting p32 A bit longer or shorter p34	Same and different p36	Ice-cream p38
D Calculating, measuring and understanding shape	Positions p40 How to pay p42	Times p44 Fun with position p46	Getting there p48 Fairground ride p50
E Securing number facts, relationships and calculating	Allsorts p52 Shells p54	Starfish p56 Feeding time p58	Counting coins p60 Ducks p62

PRIMARY FRAMEWORK COVERAGE

All the activities in this book give opportunities for children to use, apply and develop their knowledge and skills across the curriculum. They also support the development of some of the speaking, listening and group discussion objectives outlined in the *Primary Framework for literacy and mathematics*.

USING AND APPLYING MATHEMATICS	• Solve problems involving counting, adding, subtracting, doubling or halving in the context of numbers, measures or money, for example to 'pay' and 'give change'. • Describe a puzzle or problem using numbers, practical materials and diagrams; use these to solve the problem and set the solution in the original context. • Answer a question by selecting and using suitable equipment, and sorting information, shapes or objects; display results using tables and pictures. • Describe simple patterns and relationships involving numbers or shapes; decide whether examples satisfy given conditions. • Describe ways of solving puzzles and problems, explaining choices and decisions orally or using pictures.
SPEAKING	• Retell stories, ordering events using story language. • Experiment with and build new stores of words to communicate in different contexts.
LISTENING	• Listen with sustained concentration, building new stores of words in different contexts. • Listen to and follow instructions accurately, asking for help and clarification if necessary.
GROUP DISCUSSION	• Take turns to speak, listen to each other's suggestions and talk about what they are going to do. • Ask and answer questions, make relevant contributions, offer suggestions and take turns. • Explain their views to others in a small group, decide how to report the group's views to the class.

SNOWMEN

Introduction

- Load up the *Mind's Eye* CD-ROM. Ask children for an initial response to what they see.
- Discuss the snowman, asking questions such as:
  - *Have you ever made a snowman? How long did it take?*
  - *What do you need to make a snowman? What could you use for a nose if you didn't have a carrot?*
  - *Why doesn't the snowman have any legs?*
  - *What else can you build from snow?*

Discussion

- Ask related questions such as:
  - *In which season might you see a snowman? Which months are in this season?*
  - *Why don't snowmen last for very long?*
  - *Is this snowman fat or thin?*
  - *Are the buttons equally spaced? Are they the same size?*
  - *Which arm is longer?*

© Paul Tessier/iStockphoto

  - *Are there more buttons or arms? How many more?*
  - *How could you check your answer?*

Content focus

Block A, Unit 1 – solve problems involving counting

ACTIVITIES

⭐ Think, pair, share

- Tell children that their job is to use numbers to talk about the snowman.
- Ask children to think on their own about what they might say about the snowman.
- Ask pairs to sit facing each other. Partners take it in turns to share their ideas. Ask them to come up with as many statements as possible to share with the rest of the class.
- After a few minutes, ask the pairs to decide on one statement that they thought of when they talked together. Each pair should contribute something that has not already been said. Give pairs time to choose another statement if the one they chose has already been mentioned.
- Encourage children to use words like 'more' and 'fewer', prompting with questions such as: *Are there more fingers or eyes on the snowman? How many more? How do you know?*
- Compile a list of mathematical vocabulary used during the activity.

⭐ Snowballing

- Ask children to close their eyes and imagine that there are two snowmen.
- After some thinking time, ask them to join a friend to make a pair and talk about how many noses there are altogether.
- Agree as a class that there are two noses altogether.
- Pairs of children work out together the number of arms, scarves and buttons for two snowmen. The pairs then join another pair to share their solutions.
- Ask each group to make a drawing together of the two snowmen to check their answers.

AfL Can children choose an item/items to count and communicate the number accurately to the group? Can children use the terms 'more' and 'fewer' in the context of the problem?

Challenge

Ask children to make up some questions with number answers. *How many buttons, arms, etc. will three, four and five snowmen have? How can you record this?*

Move on to using logiblocks to make a snowman. *What shapes have you used? How many blocks have you used? Can you use the same blocks to make two snowmen?*

KEY VOCABULARY

count, the same number as, altogether, more, fewer, longer, shorter

Name _____   Date _____

SNOWMEN

Draw two snowmen.

Use

★ 12 buttons altogether
★ 10 fingers altogether
★ 2 hats altogether
★ 2 scarves altogether
★ 2 noses altogether

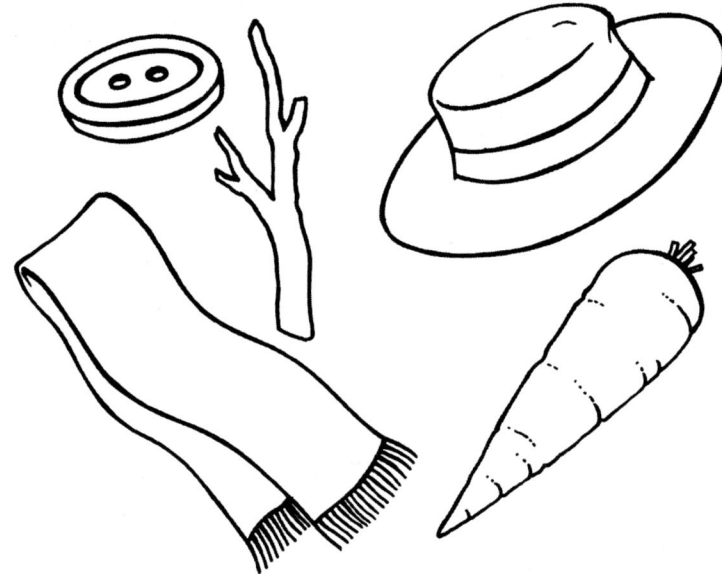

big snowman   **small snowman**

© Rising Stars UK Ltd. 2010   Mind's Eye/Talk for Maths   Book 1/SNOWMEN

COUNT AWAY

Introduction
- Load up the *Mind's Eye* CD-ROM. Ask children for an initial response to what they see.
- Discuss the rows of peas, asking questions such as: *How many peas do you think there could be?* Ensure that children estimate rather than count at this point. *Are there more peas in this row or this one? Why do you think that?*

Discussion
- Ask further questions such as:
  - *How could we find out if there are enough peas for everyone here?*
  - *Is there an equal number of peas in each row?*
  - *Does every pea have a partner?*
  - *Which row is longer/shorter?*
  - *Why is that row longer/shorter?*

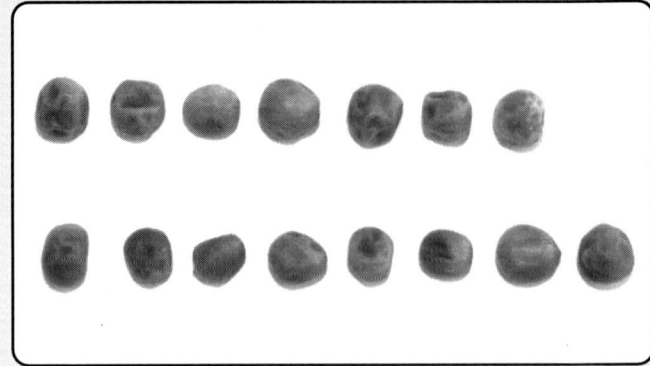

© Rising Stars UK Ltd.

Content focus
Block A, Unit 1 – solve problems involving counting

ACTIVITIES

 Snowballing

- Tell children that you want to find different ways to count the peas. Allow about a minute of thinking time. No-one should make a response until the time is up.
- After the initial thinking time, ask children to join a friend to make a pair. They spend a few minutes finding some different ways to count the peas. If they struggle to get started, encourage them to start the count from different points.
- Pairs then join with another pair to share their results. Encourage them to listen carefully to one another's methods.
- Invite children to explain their ideas to the whole class. Keep the discussion going with questions such as:
  – *What did you decide to do?*
  – *Can you explain that in a different way?*
  – *Who can say that in different way?*
  – *Who has another idea?*
  – *Which do you think is the best way? Why?*
  – *How many are there altogether?*
  – *How do you know that you have counted them all?*
  – *Does it make any difference where you start counting?*

⭐ **Think, pair, share**

- Give pairs counters. Ask them to put out 20 counters spaced as equally as possible. Partners should collaborate to ensure that they use the correct number.
- Pairs play 'one more'. Player A hides some of the counters with their hand. Player B counts the number of counters that are showing and says the number.
- Player A keeps the counters covered up. Both children work out and say the number that is one more than the number of counters that are showing. They should use full sentences, e.g. *"Eight is one more than seven"*.
- Finally, hold a discussion with the class to find the number that is 'one more than'. Use the image of the peas and cover a small number. Ask questions such as:
  – *How many peas are showing?*
  – *What if one more was showing?*
  – *How do you know that?*
  – *How can we check?*

> **AfL** Can children choose and use a way of counting the arrangement of peas accurately?
> Do children know that the number of objects does not change if you move the objects around?
> Can children say the number that is one more?

 Challenge

Encourage children to cover up some of the peas. *How could you work out how many are covered?*

KEY VOCABULARY
the same number as, as many as, equal to, more, fewer, one more than

COUNT AWAY

How many ladybirds?

Find 2 ways to count them.

Explain how you counted.

Use drawings to help.

IN MY HOME

Introduction
- Load up the *Mind's Eye* CD-ROM. Ask children for an initial response to what they see.
- The photograph is of Neuschwanstein Castle in Germany. It was built by King Ludwig II. He built it high up in the mountains far away from other towns because he was very shy. King Ludwig died before the castle was completely finished. These days more than a million people visit the castle every year. Neuschwanstein Castle was the inspiration for the castle that you see at the beginning of some Disney films. Lots of other films and even computer games use this famous castle.

© Maxim Krasnov/iStockphoto

Discussion
- This is a very unusual home for someone to live in. Hold a brief discussion about other types of homes. Invite children to tell you about their homes if they would like to.
- Move on to ask children to tell you about things they have in their homes. Keep this fairly general. Ask questions such as:
  - *Is there anything in this classroom that you have at home?*
  - *Tell me something that you have lots of at home.*

Content focus
Block A, Unit 2 – compare and order numbers

ACTIVITIES

 Home group
- Each child has a turn to tell the rest of their group about things they have in their home that fit the statements below. Encourage them to think carefully before sharing.
  - *There is one ... in my home.*
  - *There are two ... in my home.*
  - *There are less than five ... in my home.*
  - *There are more than ten ... in my home.*

Listening triangles
- Children sit in talking groups of three. Give groups a few minutes to agree upon a statement to share with the rest of the class for each of the following:
  - *There is one ... in our classroom.*
  - *There are between 20 and 30 ... in our classroom.*
  - *There are more than 20 ... in our classroom.*
  - *There are not enough ... in our classroom.*

> **AfL** Can children compare numbers up to 20 and say which number is bigger?

Challenge
Children estimate numbers in the classroom, e.g. how many pencils in the box, how many bricks on the wall?

KEY VOCABULARY
count, more, less, compare, between, how many?

Name _____ Date _____

IN MY HOME

Complete these:

There is 1 _____ in my home.

There are 2 _____ in my home.

There are more than 5 _____ in my home.

There are more than 20 _____ in my home.

There are less than 20 _____ in my home.

MAKING NUMBERS

Introduction
- Load up the *Mind's Eye* CD-ROM. Ask children for an initial response to what they see.

Discussion
- Ask children to volunteer mathematical statements using the numbers shown.
- Ask questions such as:
  - How did you work that out?
  - Can you add two numbers and then another one?
  - What if you take away instead of add?
  - What if you use three 1s instead of two?
  - How can you make a number that is greater than three?
  - How can you make six?
  - Can you count in twos, and then count on one?
  - What is the biggest number you can make?

Content focus
Block A, Unit 2 – problems involving addition and subtraction

© Rising Stars UK Ltd.

ACTIVITIES

Think, pair, share
- Children will need linking cubes, paper and pencils.
- Ask children to use 1s and 2s to make five.
- Children work individually on the problem. They can use cubes to help them work out solutions as required.
- They then join with a partner to share their solutions. Ask them to find a way to record all the ways they have found to show the class.
- Pairs share their solutions and recording with the whole class.

★ Snowballing
- Each pair will need linking cubes in two different colours.
- Children price the two colours of cubes as either 1p or 2p. Tell them they are going to make a 20p dog. Pairs talk about how to do this before starting. Encourage them to plan ahead and make jottings to show their ideas, although there is likely to be a good deal of trial and improvement in this activity.
- When pairs have made their dogs, they join with another pair and compare. They check the value of each other's dogs.
- Finally, compare all the dogs. Discuss the differences. Ask questions such as: *Why can these dogs all be worth the same, but be different sizes?*

> **AfL** Can children talk about adding and subtracting? Can children use the signs +, – and = when they write addition and subtraction sentences?

Challenge
Children make a different dog worth 20p.

KEY VOCABULARY
add, altogether, subtract, how much more?

MAKING NUMBERS

Make 10.

Use **1**   **2**   **+**   **−**   **=**

How many ways can you do it?

CAR NUMBERS

Introduction

- Load up the *Mind's Eye* CD-ROM. Ask children for an initial response to what they see.
- Explain that ever since cars were invented over a hundred years ago, every car has a vehicle registration plate (number plate) so that they can all be identified. In most parts of the world, there is a number plate at both the front and back of the car. All number plates have numbers and letters, but the way they are arranged depends on the country.
- This car number plate is on an old car in Jersey, which is an island off the coast of France. In Jersey, every number plate begins with the letter J and is followed by a set of numbers.

Discussion

- Encourage children to describe what they can see.
- Ask questions about the number plate such as:
  - *Have you ever seen a number plate with this many numbers?*
  - *How many digits are there?*
  - *Which is the largest digit?*
  - *What is the first/second/third/fourth/fifth digit?*
  - *Can anyone say the digits in order of size?*
  - *Are all the numbers from one to ten here?*
  - *Which are missing?*

© Jenny Penfold

Content focus

Block A, Unit 3 – use knowledge of place value to position numbers to 20 and beyond on a number track and number line; know addition and subtraction facts to at least 10

ACTIVITIES

 Snowballing

- Children will need sticky notes and access to a 1–100 number line.
- Children should sit four at a table.
- Children start in pairs. Ask them to make as many two-digit numbers as possible using the digits on the car number plate. They write each number on a sticky note.
- After a set period of time, perhaps five minutes, give a signal for children to stop writing numbers. Ask them to arrange the sticky notes in a line to put their numbers in order of size, starting with the smallest. They use the 0–100 number line to help them order the numbers.
- Pairs join with the other pair at the table. They compare their work to see if there are any other numbers they can make. The group of four adds in the five single-digit numbers to their sticky note numbers.

 Think, pair, share

- You can make nearly all the numbers between one and ten by adding or subtracting the numbers on the car. *Which number can't you make?* [The answer is 2.]
- Children work on the problem individually for a few minutes before joining a partner. Pairs collaborate to make the numbers from one to ten, e.g. 4 + 5 = 9, 9 – 1 = 8. Encourage them to talk about how to approach the problem and to listen to each other's ideas.
- When children have worked on the task for an appropriate time, work with the class. Write the numbers one to ten on the board. Invite children to explain how they made each number.

AfL Do children know the order of numbers to 20 and beyond? Can they write them?
Can children use their knowledge of number facts to 10 and beyond in a problem?

 Challenge

Ask children: *Which three-digit numbers could you make from the car numbers?*

KEY VOCABULARY

digit, more, first, second, third, fourth, fifth, bigger, smaller, compare, order

Name _____ Date _____

CAR NUMBERS

Draw some cars in A.

A

Draw more cars in B than in A.

B

Draw fewer cars in C than in A.

C

How many cars altogether?

© Rising Stars UK Ltd. 2010   Mind's Eye/Talk for Maths   Book 1/CAR NUMBERS

ANIMAL SUMS

Introduction
- Load up the *Mind's Eye* CD-ROM. Ask children for an initial response to what they see.
- Explain that meerkats live in the Kalahari Desert in Southern Africa. They mostly eat insects but they also eat small mammals, eggs, lizards and even scorpions. Meerkats need to eat a lot every day because their bodies are not good at storing food. When they are looking for food in a group, they have a sentry on guard while the others search for food. Meerkats have black areas around their eyes to deflect the sun's glare and help them see well on bright days so that they can avoid predators who want to eat them. They live in burrows under the ground and are good at digging into the sand. When they do this, their ears can close shut.

Discussion
- Ask if children have seen meerkats on television or in a zoo. Ask them to tell you how they move. Establish that they have four legs, although they spend quite a lot of time standing on their back legs so it looks as if they only have two.

© iStockphoto

- Ask how many tails the meerkats in the picture would have between them. Take responses and ask children to explain how they know.

Content focus
Block A, Unit 3 – solve problems involving counting and adding numbers

ACTIVITIES

⭐ Snowballing
- Children will need linking cubes.
- Ask pairs to make a model meerkat from linking cubes.
- They join with another pair to compare their meerkats. In their group of four, they estimate and write down how many cubes each meerkat is made of.
- The group tries to count how many cubes they have used without breaking their models up. They check by counting.

⭐ Talk partners
- Ask pairs to make two different model meerkats using two colours of cubes.
- They talk to each other about how they are the same and how they are different, using mathematical language, e.g. *"Mine has more black cubes than yours. This meerkat has two more yellow cubes in its tail. The tall meerkat has shorter legs. I used 16 cubes to make this meerkat."*
- Ask pairs to dismantle their meerkats and make two towers, one for each colour cube. They compare their size, talking or writing if appropriate, e.g. *"There are four more black cubes than yellow"*.

> **AfL** Can children explain how they calculated the totals?

Challenge
Children make a meerkat using 25 cubes and five different colours. They use the same number of each colour cube.

KEY VOCABULARY
add, more, plus, total, equals, one more, two more …, taller, shorter

Name _____ Date _____

ANIMAL SUMS

Draw an animal picture.

There must be 8 legs altogether.

There must be more than 1 tail.

TRIANGLES AND SQUARES

Introduction

- Load up the *Mind's Eye* CD-ROM. Ask children for an initial response to what they see.
- Ask children to share anything they might know about patchwork quilts.
- Explain that a patchwork quilt is a quilt in which the top layer is made of pieces of material sewn together to make a design. Originally, this was done to use up left-over pieces of material. The designs often use shapes with which children will be familiar. People have been quilting for a very long time. Cottages and castles were draughty places, and doorways and window openings were sometimes covered with patchwork quilts. Examples of quilting have even been found in the tombs of Egyptian Pharaohs dating back many thousands of years. Joseph's coat of many colours was probably patchwork.

Discussion

- Discuss the image. Keep the discussion moving by asking questions such as:
  - *Tell me what you can see.*
  - *How would you describe the pattern?*

© John Teate/iStockphoto

- *What shape do the four triangles in the middle make?*
- *What shape do the two red triangles make?*
- *Does it matter which way up it is?*

Content focus

Block B, Unit 1 – visualise and name 2-D shapes, describing their features

ACTIVITIES

 Think, pair, share

- Pairs will need whiteboards or paper and pens, scrap paper, scissors, pinboards and rubber bands, square and triangular 2-D shapes.
- Before children start on the activity, make sure that they are familiar with the properties of triangles and squares. Ask questions such as:
  - *What is this shape? How do you know?*
  - *Draw a triangle on your whiteboard.*
  - *How many sides/corners does each shape have?*
  - *How is the square different from the triangle?*
- Say: *Start with a triangle. How can you change it into a square?*
- Children think on their own for a few minutes. They then share their ideas with their partner. Pairs try out each other's ideas by drawing, cutting, folding or manipulating the 2-D shapes to help solve the problem.
- Hold a whole-class discussion to share ideas. These might include:
  - starting with a triangle and adding three more, fitting them together at corners
  - starting with a paper triangle and folding in the corners
  - starting with a paper triangle and cutting off the corners
  - drawing a triangle, rubbing out two sides and adding three in the correct positions
  - making a triangle on the pinboard and moving the rubber band.

 Talk partners

- Give pairs a set of triangles and squares.
- Children sit facing each other with a screen such as a large book between them so that they cannot see each other's shapes.
- They take it in turns to make a pattern with their shapes. They then tell their partner how to make the pattern. They remove the screen to see if their patterns match.

AfL Can children use 2-D and 3-D shapes to make patterns and pictures?
Can children name most of the 2-D shapes they used?

 Challenge

Look at these shapes. Listen to this description of one of them. Which shape am I describing? Children repeat with a partner.

KEY VOCABULARY

square, triangle, shape, sides, corners, next to, above, below, the same, different

Name _____   Date _____

TRIANGLES AND SQUARES

Join dots to make triangles.

Do not use a dot more than once.

Do not cross lines.

How many different triangles can you make?

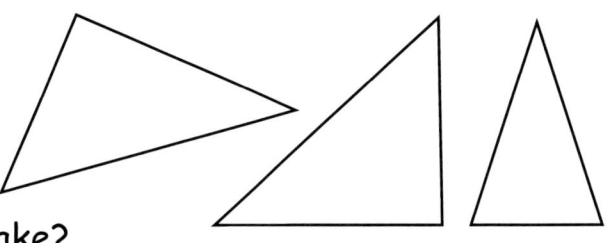

© Rising Stars UK Ltd. 2010   Mind's Eye/Talk for Maths   Book 1/TRIANGLES AND SQUARES

DOMINOES

Introduction
- Load up the *Mind's Eye* CD-ROM. Ask children for an initial response to what they see.
- Ask children to share all they know about dominoes.
- Explain that dominoes came to Europe around 400 years ago, but are originally a Chinese invention. Each domino represented one of the results of throwing two dice. One half of each domino showed the spots from one dice and the other half showed the spots from the second dice. The most popular set of dominoes has 28 pieces and includes blanks.
- Show a set of dominoes. Demonstrate how to use the dominoes. Establish that the largest number of spots on one side of the domino is six.

Discussion
- Look at the dominoes in the picture again and ask children to describe them in detail.
- Ask questions such as:
  - Count all the orange spots. Can you count them in twos?
  - Which domino has the smallest number of spots?

© Jenny Penfold

  - Are there more orange spots or more red spots?
  - How many spots altogether on the third domino?
  - Can you find a quicker way to count them?

Content focus
Block B, Unit 1 – early addition and subtraction using related language and symbols

ACTIVITIES

Hot seating
- Each group has a set of dominoes and individual whiteboards or paper.
- Demonstrate this with the whole class initially. Children sit in home groups. The teacher decides on a domino to be. Groups take turns to ask questions to help them identify which domino you are, e.g. "Do you have more than six spots?"
- Groups should agree between them which question to ask. Encourage them to discard any dominoes that do not fit the criteria so the possibilities get steadily smaller. When a group thinks they know which domino you have chosen, they draw it on a whiteboard or paper.
- Children repeat the activity, playing within their home groups.

Snowballing
- Children need whiteboards or paper.
- Children sit in pairs and discuss the addition facts they can make using the spots on the dominoes shown, e.g. 2 + 2 = 4 or 2 + 5 = 7. They record their facts.
- After a few minutes, children join another pair to compare their lists. They take it in turns to read out one of their additions, and the other pair checks to see if they have it. Each pair records any new addition facts, and the group of four tries to generate new facts.

> **AfL** Can children derive addition facts for totals to at least five and work out the corresponding subtraction facts?

Challenge
The set of dominoes in the picture has a total of 22 spots. Children make a set that has a total of 10 spots. *Can you make a smaller set with 10 spots?*

KEY VOCABULARY
add, more, equals, how many?

Name _____ Date _____

DOMINOES

Use dominoes from a full set.
Can you find where the different dominoes go?

Some go this way.　　　　Some go this way.

4	3	0
0	1	5
4	3	6
3	3	4

Mind's Eye/Talk for Maths   Book 1/DOMINOES

MONEY BOX

Introduction
- Load up the *Mind's Eye* CD-ROM. Ask children for an initial response to what they see.
- Explain that piggy banks or money boxes are for saving small coins. They don't have to be pig-shaped. About 500 years ago, jars were made out of a special clay called 'pygg'. Whenever anyone could save an extra coin, they put it into one of their clay jars. They called this their pygg bank. These days many pots for savings are pig-shaped. The money can be put in easily and, in the traditional type of bank, you have to break open the pig to get the money out. Many piggy banks have a rubber stopper in the bottom so that you don't have to break them. Some people like to collect piggy banks.

Discussion
- Discuss whether children have started to save. *Do you spend your money as soon as you are given any or do you save it?*
- Ask children to tell you about the coins we use. Remind children of their equivalences as appropriate. Highlight the usefulness of being able to count in twos, fives and tens.

© Felix Möckel/iStockphoto

- Ask questions such as:
  - How many 2p coins are needed to make 12p?
  - Can you find a quicker way to work that out?
  - How can you make 20p with one coin/two coins?
  - How do you know that it is correct?

Content focus
Block B, Unit 2 – problems involving money

ACTIVITIES

 Snowballing
- Children will need coins and a whiteboard or paper.
- Imagine there are four different coins in the piggy bank. *How much money could there be?* Hold a joint discussion to get things moving, inviting children to tell you an amount that could be in the piggy bank and the coins that would be used.
- Children work in pairs, initially discussing how to go about solving the problem before trying to find as many amounts as possible.
- Encourage children to work systematically. They keep track of their solutions on their whiteboard or paper, showing how they make each amount.
- After a few minutes, pairs join to make groups of four. They compare their solutions and come up with a joint list showing how much money there could be.

 Rainbowing
- Children start in groups of three. They start a list of the amounts that could be in the piggy bank using:
  - the same coin
  - two different coins
  - three different coins
  - four different coins.
- After a few minutes, give each group member a different colour. Children move into single-colour groups and share their work with their new group members.
- In their new groups, children make a poster showing their findings.

> **AfL** Can children add and subtract some numbers in their heads?
> Do children use the values of the coins correctly when working out totals?

Challenge
Children work on this problem. *Joe has three coins. They are worth between 15p and 25p altogether. How much money could Joe have? Explain why.*

KEY VOCABULARY
answer, money, coin, pence, pound, total, what could we try next?

MONEY BOX

How much money does Femi have?

She has less than 25p. She has no pennies.

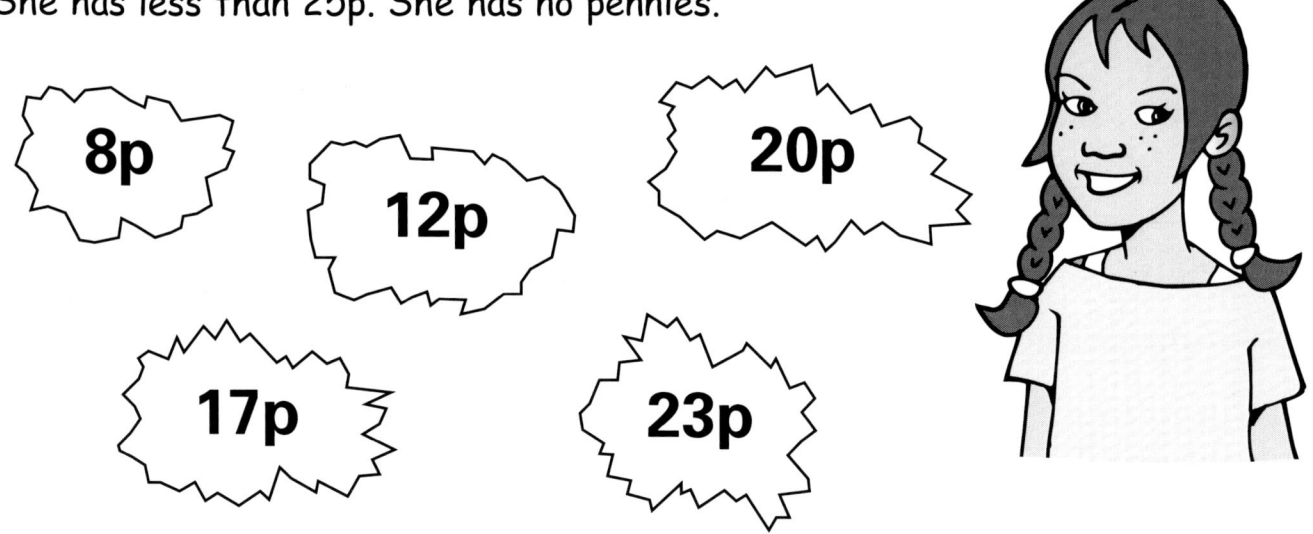

Put a ring around an answer. Draw coins to show how you know.

WOULD YOU RATHER?

Introduction
- Load up the *Mind's Eye* CD-ROM. Ask children for an initial response to what they see.
- Ask children what they think coins are made of. Explain that most coins are made of a mixture of metals. Copper is one of the main metals because it helps to make other metals harder. Coins are handled by lots of people, and passing coins from one person to another could spread germs, but copper is special because it is antibacterial. This means that any germs that have been on someone's hands are poisoned and are less likely to spread.

Discussion
- Discuss the picture of the coins. *What coins can you see? Which pile of coins is higher?*

© Rising Stars UK Ltd.

Content focus
Block B, Unit 2 – problems involving money

ACTIVITIES

Rainbowing
- Remind children of the story *Would You Rather?* by John Burningham in which lots of funny choices are given. Read the book together if possible.
- Groups of three children talk about which pile of money in the picture they would rather have and give their reasons. They take turns to speak. Encourage them to discuss their reasons with each other.
- After a few minutes, allocate group members the colour blue, yellow or red. Children form new single-colour groups to come to a joint decision about which pile of coins they would rather have.
- Ask each group to draw a picture to show something they would like to buy with the coins they would rather have.

⭐ Snowballing
- Give children this problem. *Joe says "I have more money than you" and Polly answers "No you don't! I have more coins".*
- Children discuss the problem in pairs. When they think they have a solution, they join up with another pair to compare their ideas. Groups of four then combine their ideas.
- Bring the class together. Ask the class for suggestions as to what Polly could say to Joe.
- Encourage children to explain how they worked on the problem. Ask questions like: *What did you do first? Is there another way? Can Joe have more money if he has fewer coins? Why? What is worth more – one 5p coin or two 2p coins?*

> **AfL** Can children explain how to work out the value of the two piles of coins?

Challenge
Give children this problem. *There are three 10p coins, three pennies and two 5p coins in a money box. If you shake out four coins, what is the smallest amount you can get? What is the largest amount?*

KEY VOCABULARY
answer, money, coin, pence, pound, total, most, least, how much?

Name _____ Date _____

WOULD YOU RATHER?

Is there enough money to buy the toy?

What coins do you need?

Work out some different ways to pay for it.

PATTERNS

Introduction

- Load up the *Mind's Eye* CD-ROM. Ask children for an initial response to what they see.
- Explain that sweets like this are made from melted sugar, honey, etc. with added flavourings. They are then heated up and colouring is added. They are put into moulds to cool.
- Discuss the colours of the sweets and what they might taste of.

Discussion

- Continue the discussion. Ask questions such as:
  - *Are the sweets arranged in a regular pattern?*
  - *Can you see a pattern in the colours?*
  - *How many sweets do you think there are?*
- Establish that this is a random arrangement with no repeating pattern.

© Eric Willner

Content focus

Block B, Unit 2 – describe simple patterns and relationships

ACTIVITIES

Think, pair, share

- Children will need linking cubes.
- Give children a few minutes to work on this problem individually: *Make a stick of yellow and blue cubes. Start with yellow, then blue and keep going. What colour will cubes number 6, 10 and 20 be?*
- Children join with a partner to discuss this problem and work out a joint solution before checking it with cubes. Encourage them to model the problem using cubes. If some children are unable to visualise the solution, they should find a way to record their thoughts as jottings.
- Pairs share solutions and discuss methods with the whole class.

★ Snowballing

- Children work together in pairs to make a pattern stick 18 cubes long from red, black and orange cubes. The fifth cube must be black. The colours must make a regular pattern.
- Children should talk about how they are going to tackle the problem before they touch the cubes. Encourage them to sit on their hands if they find this difficult.
- After making their pattern stick, pairs join to make groups of four. They discuss what is the same about their pattern sticks and what is different. They describe each other's patterns.

AfL Can children use numbers or shapes to make patterns of their own and describe their patterns to others ?

Challenge

If you wrote the numbers 1, 2, 3, 4 ... up to 50, would you write more 1s or more 9s?

KEY VOCABULARY

pattern, repeat, another, regular, same, different

Name _____ Date _____

PATTERNS

Draw the missing shapes in this pattern.

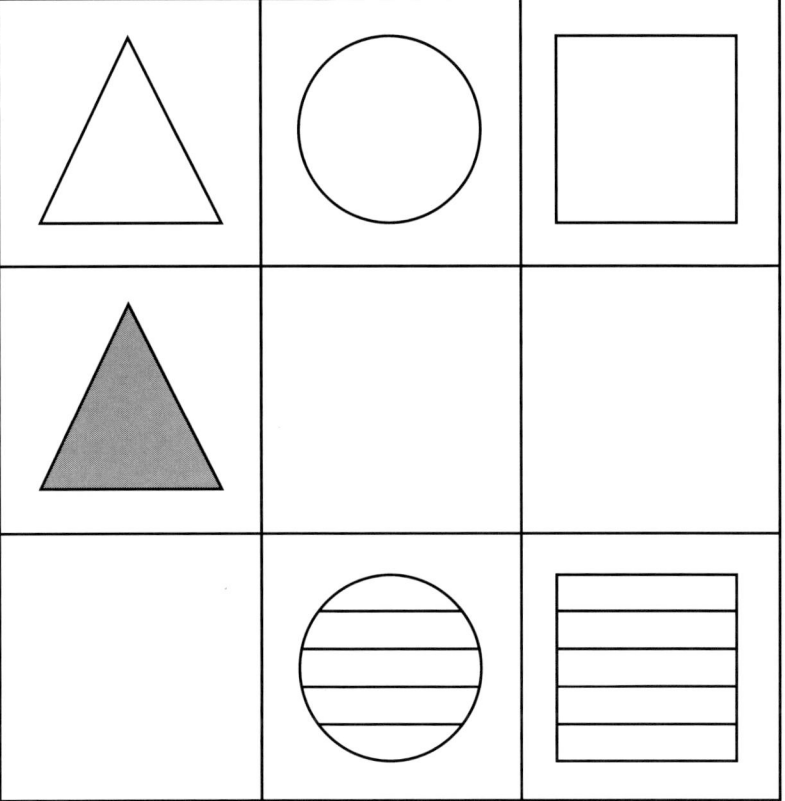

Make up your own pattern.

AIRBRICK PATTERNS

Introduction

- Load up the *Mind's Eye* CD-ROM. Ask children for an initial response to what they see.
- Explain that an airbrick is a block with holes that is put into a wall. It lets the air travel through it so that the wall doesn't get damp. They can be made of clay, steel or plastic. In old houses you can sometimes see airbricks made of heavy cast iron with interesting patterns. This is quite an unusual brick because they are usually rectangular.

Discussion

- Invite children to describe what they can see.
- Ask questions such as:
  - *What shape is the airbrick?*
  - *What shapes can you see inside the airbrick?*
  - *How would you describe the pattern?*
  - *How could you make this pattern with shapes in the classroom?*

© Rudi Tapper/iStockphoto

Content focus

Block B, Unit 3 – visualise and name common 2-D shapes and 3-D solids, describing their features; use them to make patterns, pictures and models

ACTIVITIES

Snowballing

- Children will need 2-D shapes – circles, squares, rectangles, triangles (including isosceles triangles), pentagons, hexagons.
- Children start in pairs. Tell children that they are going to use some shapes to make a pattern for an airbrick. Remind children that airbricks can be square or rectangular. All the shapes they use must have less than five sides. Ask pairs to sort out the shapes together so that they have the correct ones to use for the task.
- Each pair makes a pattern for an airbrick using the shapes. At a given signal, pairs join to make fours. They compare their patterns. Each pair says three ways in which their patterns are similar and three ways in which they are different.
- Ask each pair to rearrange the shapes used by the other pair to make a new pattern.

Home group

- Children will need squares of sticky coloured paper, scissors, pencils and rulers.
- Ask every child in the group to draw a straight line across a square to divide it into two pieces and then cut the pieces out.
- Children take turns to describe the shapes they have made to the group. They repeat with a new square, working as a group to find what other shapes they can make with one cut.
- The group works together to make a chart showing the shapes they can make with one cut.

> **AfL** Can children use shapes to make patterns of their own and explain what comes next?
> Can children sort shapes according to a given rule?

Challenge

Ask children to draw two lines across a square and then cut along the lines. *How many pieces do you have? What shapes are they? What other shapes could you make with two cuts?*

KEY VOCABULARY

shape, make, triangle, circle, rectangle, square, sort

Name _____ Date _____

AIRBRICK PATTERNS

Use the clues to find the card.

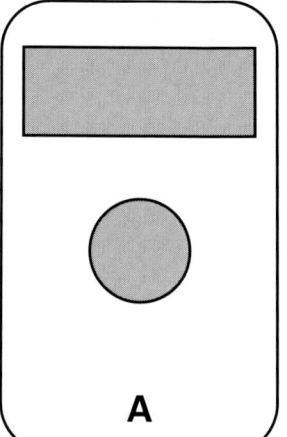
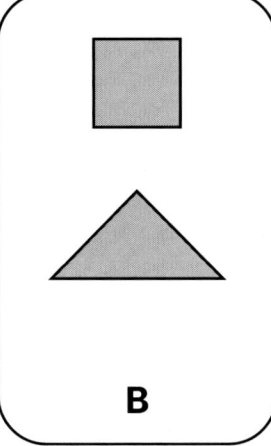
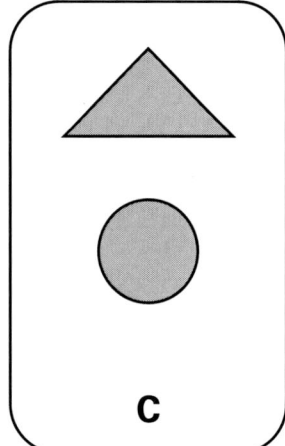
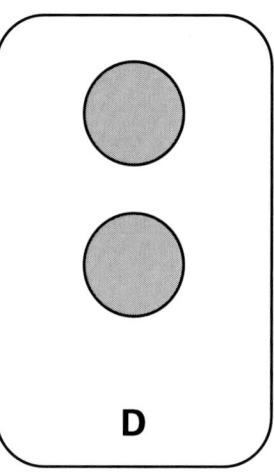

A B C D

Clues

★ There is a circle on the card.

★ One of the shapes is not a circle.

★ One of the shapes has 4 corners.

The card is _____ .

Draw your own cards. Write clues.

CUPCAKES

Introduction
- Load up the *Mind's Eye* CD-ROM. Ask children for an initial response to what they see.
- Explain that cupcakes, also called fairy cakes, are small cakes that are made for one person to eat. Over 200 years ago, cupcakes were baked in cups, giving them their name. They are now baked in a small paper cup. Cupcakes cook much more quickly than standard-sized cakes because they are small. The recipe for cupcakes can be measured out with one cupful each of eggs, sugar, flour and butter. This may be another reason for their name.

Discussion
- Invite children to describe what they can see. *What flavours could the cakes be?* Which one would you like to eat? Encourage them to talk about making cakes, for example at school.
- Ask questions such as:
  - How many cupcakes are on the plate?
  - Are there enough for ten children to have a cake each?
  - How many more would we need?

© Ruth Black/iStockphoto

- If someone has already eaten two cakes, how many were there before?

Content focus
Block B, Unit 3 – solve problems involving adding and subtracting; count on in steps of 3 or 4 from zero, or from any small number

ACTIVITIES

Envoy
- Children will need access to counters, a number line and strips of paper.
- Say: *Twelve cakes. Five are big. How many are little?*
- Children answer the question in their group. It is the responsibility of all group members to try to ensure that everyone understands by finding a way to explain or model the answer.
- Ask each group to make up some more questions that use subtraction. They write the questions on strips of paper. The questions can be asked about any number of cupcakes.
- When each group has found a few possibilities, choose group envoys. The envoys collect a question from a different group and bring it back to their home group to answer.

⭐ Snowballing
- Give children this problem. *Emma had some boxes of cakes. Some boxes had three cakes. Some boxes had four cakes. Altogether Emma's boxes had 19 cakes. How many boxes had three cakes in?*
- Children start by working on the problem in pairs. Encourage them to think about how many cakes Emma might have if she just has the boxes that contain three cakes.
- Ask pairs to talk about how to use what they have learned to find out which combinations of boxes will contain 19 cakes.
- Children work on the problem. When they have a solution, they join another pair and compare ideas. *Can pairs find two correct answers to the problem?*

> **AfL** Can children use mathematical words and symbols to describe and record addition and subtraction calculations?

Challenge
Give children this problem. *There are ten cakes on a plate. Tara eats three cakes. Lee eats three more cakes than Tara. How many cakes are left?*

KEY VOCABULARY
add, plus (+), makes, sum, total, altogether, subtract, how many more to make …?

Name _____ Date _____

CUPCAKES

There are 6 cupcakes in this box.

★ Some have cream on top.
★ 2 have no cream.

How many cakes have cream?

Make up a question like this.

© Rising Stars UK Ltd. 2010   Mind's Eye/Talk for Maths   Book 1/CUPCAKES

SHAPES AND PATTERNS

Introduction

- Load up the *Mind's Eye* CD-ROM. Ask children for an initial response to what they see.
- Explain that the photograph shows a section of a knitted scarf. Knitting can be done by hand or machine. There are lots of ways to knit by hand using different sorts of wool and needles that make different patterns and textures. You can even do a special type of knitting with circular needles to make a tube (a sock would be made in this way).

Discussion

- Invite children to describe what they can see. *Have any of you tried knitting? Does anyone have a jumper that has been knitted for them?*
- Ask questions such as:
  – *Is there a pattern?*
  – *What do we know about a pattern?*
  – *Do the colours repeat? Say the colours in the order that you see them.*
  – *Is anyone here wearing patterned clothing?*
  – *What shape are the stripes?*
  – *What other shapes could be used to make a pattern?*

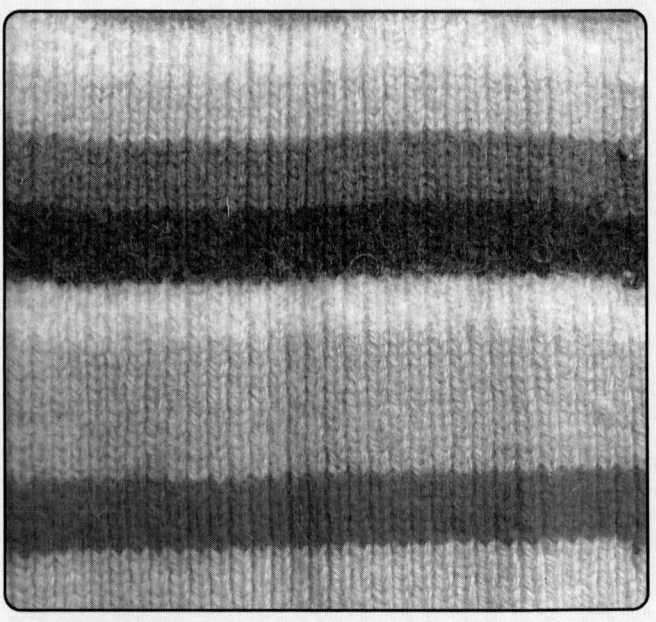

© Eric Willner

Content focus

Block B, Unit 3 – visualise and name common 2-D shapes; use them to make patterns, pictures and models

ACTIVITIES

 Talk partners

- Each pair will need a feely bag and a set of squares, triangles, circles, rectangles, cubes and spheres.
- Children put all the shapes in the bag. Taking turns, the first child takes a shape out of the bag while their partner closes their eyes. The first child keeps the shape hidden while their partner asks questions to help them identify the shape.
- After three questions have been asked and answered, the guesser must say what they think the shape is.

 Home group

- Each group will need a selection of gummed paper shapes including triangles, squares and rectangles of different sizes.
- The group makes a joint picture or pattern using the shapes. Children take turns to place a shape. As they do this, they identify the shape and say a statement about its position, e.g. *The triangle is below the square. The square is touching a smaller square.*
- When the group agrees that the picture is complete, children stick down the shapes.
- Each group nominates a member to present their picture. Groups share their work with the whole class.
- Invite children from other groups to compare the pictures using mathematical language.

AfL Can children identify and describe squares, circles, rectangles, triangles, cubes and spheres? Can children use everyday language to describe positions of shapes?

 Challenge

Ask children to write down everything they know about squares and triangles. Compare lists.

KEY VOCABULARY

shape, make, straight, solid, flat, side, corner, point, face, edge, cube, cylinder, sphere, triangle, circle, rectangle, square

SHAPES AND PATTERNS

Draw 2 scarves.

Each must have a different repeating pattern.

SORTING

Introduction
- Load up the *Mind's Eye* CD-ROM. Ask children for an initial response to what they see.
- Explain that nuts are seeds that are covered with a hard shell. Most are the seeds of trees. Nuts are useful as part of a healthy diet. Nuts can be added to sweet dishes, cakes and biscuits, as well as being an ingredient in savoury food. They are also good to eat as healthy snacks. They help to make bodies strong. A small number of people cannot eat them because nuts make them very ill.

Discussion
- Establish that there are lots of different sorts of nuts. Invite children to tell you the names of any nuts that they know or have eaten.
- Ask questions such as:
  - *Does anyone recognise any of these nuts?*
  - *Who can see a walnut?*
  - *Can anyone see an almond?*
  - *How do you know that none of these nuts are peanuts?*
  - *How many different sorts of nuts can you see?*
  - *How could we sort these nuts?*

© Eric Willner

Content focus
Block C, Unit 1 – sort information and communicate findings

ACTIVITIES

Snowballing
- Children will need an assortment of nuts (or other objects such as leaves, soft toys or pencils of different colours and lengths).
- Children work in pairs to discuss the similarities and differences between the nuts in the photograph. Encourage them to focus on colour, size and shape.
- Ask pairs to find a way to sort the nuts (or other object chosen). They decide on two sentences to tell the class about their sets, e.g. *"We have made a set of smooth nuts and a set of scratchy nuts; there are more nuts in this set than this one"*.
- Pairs join to make fours. They tell each other their sentences. Each child tries to remember one of the new pair's sentences to tell the class.

⭐ Talk partners
- This activity can be carried out with mini sorting toys as an alternative to using nuts.
- Children look at the toys and visualise a set mentally. In pairs, they take turns to sort their set but add a toy that is not a member of the set. Their partner looks at the set and explains what needs to be done to make the set correct before making the correction physically.

> **AfL** Can children describe the different ways they have sorted objects?
> Can children suggest a different criterion for grouping the same objects?

Challenge
Children use a Venn diagram to sort monsters, e.g. those with spiky hair, a green face, both or neither.

> **KEY VOCABULARY**
> sort, same, different, set, group

Name ______________________________ Date ________________

SORTING

Draw a set of monsters and put them on the Venn diagram.

All but one must have spiky hair.

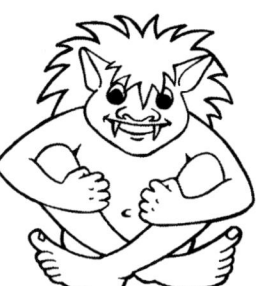

A BIT LONGER OR SHORTER

Introduction
- Load up the *Mind's Eye* CD-ROM. Ask children for an initial response to what they see.
- Remind children of the song *Tommy Thumb, Tommy Thumb, Where Are You?*. Introduce the index finger, middle finger, ring finger and little finger.
- The human hand has 27 bones. This is one more than the foot which has 26. We can grasp and pick up things because we can fold our fingers over the palm.

Discussion
- Ask children to describe the photograph in detail.
- Talk about the relative lengths of fingers. Ask questions such as:
  – Which is your left hand?
  – Show me your little finger.
  – Are all your fingers the same length?
  – Which is the longest?
  – Which is the shortest?

© Beata Becla/iStockphoto

  – Is your middle finger shorter than your thumb?
  – Is your middle finger longer than the person's next to you?

Content focus
Block C, Unit 1 – measure and compare lengths

ACTIVITIES

Snowballing
- Children will need whiteboards or paper and pencil.
- Ask children to look at their little finger and think of something longer than it. Pairs then discuss things that are just a bit longer than their little fingers. Children will need to come to an agreement about what 'a bit longer' means.
- Ask pairs to make a list using words or drawings of their ideas. The pairs join another pair to share their ideas.
- Ask the larger group to agree a joint list of things that are much longer than their little fingers.

★ Rainbowing
- Children will need sticky notes and pencils.
- Give each child in a group of four a colour to remember.
- The group agrees on some things that are a lot shorter than everyone's middle finger. Children each make a record of these things, writing or drawing each item on a separate sticky note.
- Children move to single-colour groups of no more than four and share their answers, listening carefully to each other's contributions. They use the sticky notes as prompts.
- Single-colour groups put the sticky notes in ascending order of size. They will need to decide whether to order the sticky notes by the size of the drawing or the original object of which it is a record.

> **AfL** Can children tell you how they would compare the lengths of different-sized fingers?

Challenge
Children estimate how many sticky notes long their foot is and find a way to check.

KEY VOCABULARY
long, short, longer, shorter, measure

Name _____   Date _____

A BIT LONGER OR SHORTER

Draw or write 3 things that are shorter than your foot.

Draw or write 3 things that are longer than your foot.

Draw or write 3 things that are shorter than your little finger.

Draw or write 3 things that are longer than your little finger.

SAME AND DIFFERENT

Introduction
- Load up the *Mind's Eye* CD-ROM. Ask children for an initial response to what they see.
- Explain that a clown's job is to make people laugh. There have been clowns for thousands of years, all around the world. There are always clowns in circuses. These clowns might also do things like juggling, walking the tightrope or riding horses. Different sorts of clowns wear different kinds of outfits and have special kinds of make-up. For example, some clowns, called 'whitefaces', always have white faces and red ears while others paint their faces red and outline their mouths with white paint. When top clowns join the special clown club, they paint an egg with their individual face design.

Discussion
- Discuss why the children in the photo might be dressing up as clowns.
- Ask children to describe what they see in as much detail as possible. Encourage them to talk about similarities and differences. Ask questions such as:
  – What is the same about these clowns?
  – How have their faces been painted?

© Ivonne Wierink van Wetten/iStockphoto

  – How is their hair the same/different?
  – Can you describe the blue-haired clown's outfit?
  – Tell me about the red-haired clown's lollipop.
  – How is it the same as the other lollipop? How is it different?

Content focus
Block C, Unit 2 – sort information according to a given criterion

ACTIVITIES

★ Think, pair, share
- Invite various children to say one thing about themselves.
- Tell children that they are going to talk with a friend about ways they are the same and ways they are different.
- Children sit with a partner and discuss how they are alike. Encourage them to talk about what they enjoy as well as physical features. After discussion, they agree on three sentences that begin *"We are both ..."* or *"We both like ..."*. They record their findings in a sorting diagram.
- Talk partners then discuss how they are different from each other, coming up with three differences.
- Finally, pairs tell the whole group the three ways they are alike and the three ways they are different.

★ Talk partners
- Children will need pattern blocks, logiblocks or other 2-D shapes.
- Both children in a pair choose a set of five identical shapes. At a signal from you, everyone makes a pattern with their shapes.
- Talk partners then compare their patterns. Encourage them to use positional language in their discussion.

AfL Can children suggest criteria for sorting?

⚠ Challenge
Children draw various clown faces with red hair, green hair, red noses, white faces, not white faces. They cut them out and find different ways to sort them.

KEY VOCABULARY
sort, groups, set, same, different

Name _____   Date _____

SAME AND DIFFERENT

Sam, Josh, Kai and Mikey saw some clowns.

★ Mikey saw more clowns than Sam.
★ Kai saw 2 more clowns than Josh.
★ Sam saw 10 clowns.

Write their names in the chart.

Name	Number of clowns
	12 clowns
	7 clowns
	10 clowns
	11 clowns

© Rising Stars UK Ltd. 2010   Mind's Eye/Talk for Maths   Book 1/SAME AND DIFFERENT

ICE-CREAM

Introduction
- Load up the *Mind's Eye* CD-ROM. Ask children for an initial response to what they see.
- Explain that ice-cream is usually made with dairy ingredients like milk and cream, mixed with sugar and other ingredients such as fruit. To make it nice and smooth, the mixture is stirred while it freezes. Ice-cream became popular about 70 years ago when fridges were invented because this meant that the ice-cream could be kept cold.

Discussion
- Invite children to describe what they can see. Discuss the picture, asking questions such as:
  - *How many different flavours are here?*
  - *Which is your favourite?*
  - *If there was a chocolate ice-cream next to the strawberry ice-cream, what would the next flavour be?*
  - *What other flavours are there?*

© Thomas Perkins/iStockphoto

Content focus
Block C, Unit 3 – answer a question by recording information in lists and tables; present outcomes using practical resources, pictures, block graphs or pictograms

ACTIVITIES

★ Whole class
- Establish how many children are present by counting together. Write the number on the board.
- Discuss whether everyone is at school today. *How many would there be if no-one was away?*

★ Home group
- Children will need sticky notes.
- Ask children to discuss with their home groups which of the ice-cream flavours in the picture will be most and least popular. Each child should have a turn to give their opinion. They should try to think beyond their own preference. Encourage them to talk about what other people they know like.
- Ask groups to decide how many children in the class will like strawberry, chocolate or vanilla ice-cream best. *What do you already know that will help you decide?*
- Remembering that their predictions must add up to the number present, each group writes the number of children in the class that they think prefers strawberry, chocolate or vanilla on separate sticky notes.
- Ask groups to share their predictions by putting their sticky notes under headings written on the board. Ask children to put the predictions in order under each heading. Invite children to talk about the difference in their predictions. *Why could your numbers be so different?*
- Discuss with the class how they can find out which predictions are best, aiming to agree to have a class vote. Use a show of hands to find out children's favourite flavours. Children make a class block graph using the interactive whiteboard or data software.
- Groups compare the graph with their predictions. Ask questions such as:
  - *Did your group think that more or fewer children would like chocolate?*
  - *Which ice-cream is the most popular?*
  - *Will that flavour still be the most popular when everyone is here?*
  - *Can you explain why?*
- Finally tell groups to make a list of questions that they would like to ask the class.

AfL Can children respond to questions about data they have collected?
Can children talk about which set has most?

⚠ Challenge
Ask children how else they could show their results.

KEY VOCABULARY
collect, vote, chart, compare, more, less, fewer, block graph

Name _____   Date _____

ICE-CREAM

Each ice-cream cone has a chocolate, strawberry and vanilla scoop.

Show the different ways to have the ice-cream.

What if there were 4 scoops?

POSITIONS

Introduction

- Load up the *Mind's Eye* CD-ROM. Ask children for an initial response to what they see.
- Explain that this is a picture showing some of the most important things about the country of Ecuador in South America. Show this on a globe if appropriate. Point out the snow-capped volcano and high mountains (the Andes), condors flying in the sky, men in national dress wearing ponchos and panama hats, and the llama. The stylised flowers are roses, which are sold all around the world. Point out the scarecrow. Explain that all over the world people make scarecrows to try to keep birds from eating the crops growing in fields. Ask children to tell you about the differences between the scarecrow in the painting and scarecrows they have seen in real life or on television.

Discussion

- Reinforce positional language by asking questions such as:
  - *Who is sitting next to you?*
  - *Is anyone behind you? Who?*
  - *Who is sitting between X and X?*
  - *Tell me something that is on the carpet.*
  - *What is next to the sand tray?*
  - *What is above the whiteboard?*

Content focus

Block D, Unit 1 – visualise and use everyday language to describe the position of objects

ACTIVITIES

★ Listening triangles

- You need sticky notes for the listener.
- Children should be able to see the picture clearly during this activity.
- Write these words on the board:
  next to   above   below
  in front of   behind   between
- The task is to describe the position of three things in the picture using some of these words.
- Children sit in groups of three. One person acts as the listener. The listener makes sure that the other two children use three different words to make up sentences about three things in the picture. The listener writes words or draws pictures on the sticky notes to help remember the ideas. Invite listeners to report back to the class about their listening triangle's ideas. Listeners could stick their notes below the words to generate further ideas.

★ Whole class

- Children should be able to see the picture clearly during this activity.
- Children take it in turns to give clues about something in the picture. Encourage them to use positional language, e.g. *"I'm looking at something that is higher than the volcano"* or *"This person is in front of the llama"*.
- When children think they know the answer, invite them to show the class on the screen. Before they do so, you could ask them to describe the thing in detail.

AfL Can children describe where something is using words such as next to, in front of, underneath, on top of?

❗ Challenge

Encourage children to draw a scene showing their house and to write statements about the position of things.

KEY VOCABULARY

next to, above, below, between, in front of, behind, underneath, corner, between, behind, higher, lower

Name _____ Date _____

POSITIONS

Draw a table.

★ Draw a cat on the table.
★ Draw a dog under the table.
★ Draw a bone next to the dog.

HOW TO PAY

Introduction

- Load up the *Mind's Eye* CD-ROM. Ask children for an initial response to what they see.
- Explain that these sweets are being sold in a market. Establish the difference between a shop and a market. Discuss the difference between buying sweets in a packet and buying them loose. Explain that you can choose the exact number to buy if they are sold as in the picture.
- Discuss when (and if) children buy sweets. Talk about why the dentist might advise them not to eat lots of sweets.
- Talk about healthy snacks. What are children's favourite healthy snacks?

Discussion

- Discuss the image, asking questions such as:
  - *What do your favourite sweets cost?*
  - *How many can you buy with your pocket money?*
  - *How could you pay for a blue fish that costs 7p?*
  - *Do you think this is a good way to sell sweets? Why?*
  - *How many rows of sweets can you see?*

© Carmen Martínez Banús/iStockphoto

Content focus

Block D, Unit 1 – solve problems involving counting, adding, subtracting in the context of money

ACTIVITIES

★ Think, pair, share

- Ask children what coins they know. Highlight 1p, 2p and 5p at this point, while valuing other contributions.
- Tell children that Sami bought a candy whirl. It cost 5p and she paid for it exactly.
- Ask children to work out on their own which coins she used without writing anything down at this point.
- Ask pairs to sit facing each other. Children take it in turns to explain to each other how they decided to pay for the candy whirl. Children work together to find as many ways as they can to pay 5p for the candy whirl.

★ Talk partners

- Ask pairs to draw a picture showing all the ways that Sami could pay 5p for a candy whirl. [There are four.]
- Hold a group discussion about children's solutions, using coins on a whiteboard to record. Encourage children to take turns to speak and to listen to each other carefully. Keep the discussion moving with questions such as:
  - *Did anyone else find the same way?*
  - *Who has found a different way?*
  - *How many coins does that use?*
  - *Has anyone found a way to pay 5p using fewer coins?*
  - *Which way uses the most coins?*
  - *Is 2p + 2p + 1p worth the same as 1p + 2p + 2p? Why?*
  - *Can you pay 5p using only 2p pieces?*

> **AfL** Do children know the equivalences of small coins?
> Can children pay small amounts accurately?

⚠ Challenge

Give children this problem. *Sherbet sticks cost 6p. How many ways do you think there are to make 6p? Check by working it out.*

KEY VOCABULARY

guess how many, not enough, more, fewer, most, fewest, same way, different way, how many?

HOW TO PAY

★ Sherbet dips cost 7p.
　How many ways can you pay for one?

★ A twirl costs 7p. Kai paid with 6 coins.
　Which coins did Kai use?

★ How many ways can you pay for a 10p sweet?

★ Make up a question!

　_____ coins altogether make 7p.
　Which coins?

TIMES

Introduction
- Load up the *Mind's Eye* CD-ROM. Ask children for an initial response to what they see.
- Outline the major events in a puppy's life, stressing the timeline. When puppies are born, they spend most of their time sleeping. When they are born, they can smell, but their eyes are shut. About two weeks after they are born, puppies usually begin to growl, bite, wag their tails and bark. Their food is their mother's milk until they are about two months old. Puppies, like children, need to have vaccinations to stop them getting serious diseases. Once they have had all their injections at about four months, they can meet and play with other puppies and dogs.

Discussion
- Discuss what time of day this photograph could have been taken. Encourage children to use appropriate time vocabulary.
- Ask questions such as:
  - *How long do you think it will be before the puppy wakes up?*
  - *What time do you think this puppy wakes up in the morning?*

© iStockphoto

- *How long do you think he will stay awake until his next sleep?*
- *How long do you think he will sleep in the afternoon?*
- *How long might he take to eat his next meal?*

Content focus
Block D, Unit 2 – use vocabulary related to time; order events

ACTIVITIES

★ Home group
- Prepare four strips of paper for each group of four children. Write one of the following statements on each strip:
  - brush your teeth
  - read a book
  - hop three times
  - eat school lunch.
- Each group member takes a statement and reads it aloud.
- The group discusses the statements and comes to an agreement about their order. They start with the one that takes the shortest time to carry out and finish with the action that takes the longest.
- Groups share their work with the class, justifying their choices.

★ Snowballing
- Children will need whiteboards or paper and pens.
- Ask children to plan their perfect day.
- Children decide what they will do at various times of day to enjoy themselves. They should include some meals and decide what food they will eat.
- Pairs join to make fours and share their perfect days.

AfL Can children talk about what happens at key points during the day?

⚠ Challenge
Children talk to a partner about 3 o'clock and 9 o'clock. *What do you do at these times of day and night?*

KEY VOCABULARY
time, morning, afternoon, evening, night, bedtime, before, after

Name _____ Date _____

TIMES

Draw a time on each clock.

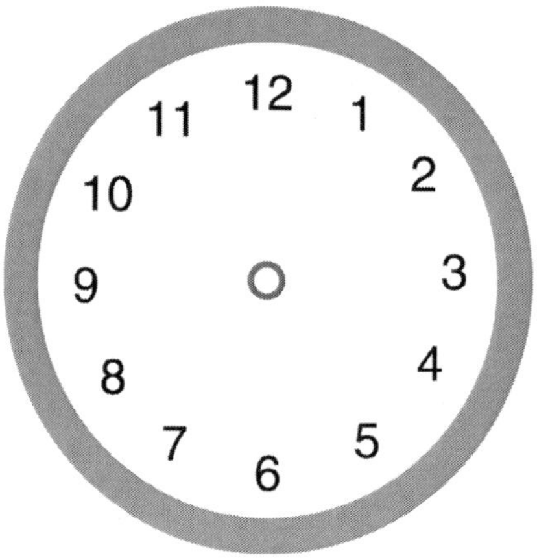

| Morning | Afternoon | Night |

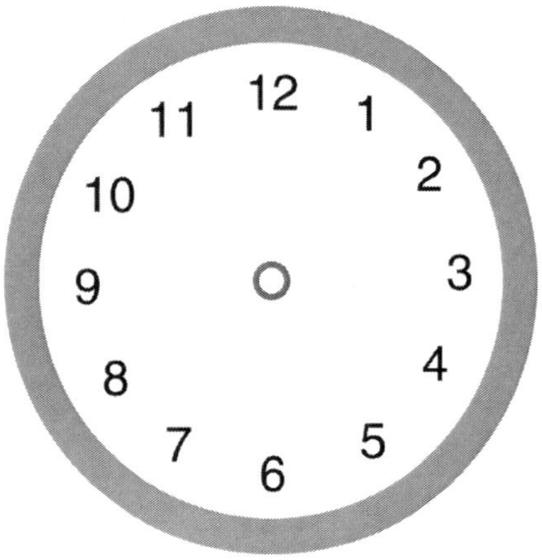

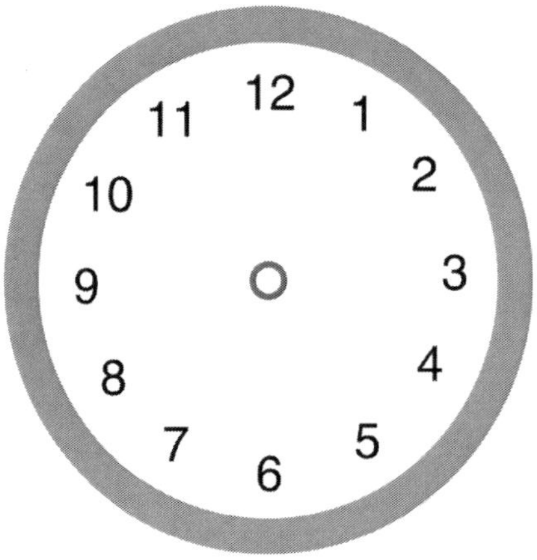

Write the time on each clock here.

_____ _____ _____

Now write 2 things you can do at each time.

Morning _____

_____

Afternoon _____

_____

Night _____

_____

© Rising Stars UK Ltd. 2010   Mind's Eye/Talk for Maths Book 1/TIMES

FUN WITH POSITION

Introduction
- Load up the *Mind's Eye* CD-ROM. Ask children for an initial response to what they see.
- Explain that the game of Snakes and Ladders was invented in India by teachers to help children learn about what might happen if they did good things or bad things. Even a hundred years ago, some Snakes and Ladders boards showed children doing good or bad deeds. The American version of the game is called Chutes and Ladders.
- Ask children to tell you what they know about the game of Snakes and Ladders.
- Establish the rules.

Discussion
- Ask questions such as:
  - *In which direction do the counters move?*
  - *How many squares are there on the board?*
  - *How many squares are there in each row?*
  - *What do you notice about the numbers in each column?*
  - *Can we use the board to help us count up in tens from 1, 2, 5, 10?*
  - *Which colour is winning this game?*

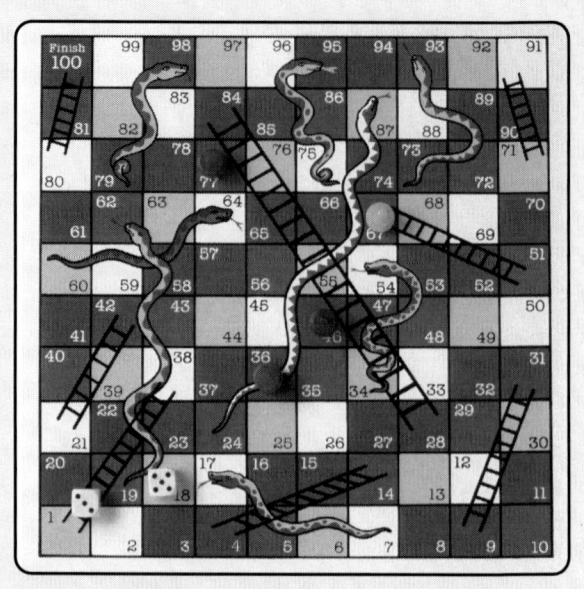

© Dorling Kindersley

- *Which is the longest snake? Where does it start/finish?*

Content focus
Block D, Unit 2 – reasoning about position, direction and movement; relate addition to counting on

ACTIVITIES

★ Think, pair, share
- Children will need access to a 1–100 number line and whiteboards or paper and pens.
- Establish with the whole group the number and position of each coloured counter in the game of Snakes and Ladders shown. Write them on the board.
- Say: *What number does green need to throw to catch up with blue?*
- Children work on the problem individually for a few minutes before joining a partner to discuss how they could find out. They then work on their solution together. One child writes the answer and the second child jots down their strategy.
- When pairs have completed the task, work with the whole class. Ask children to hold up their answers. Choose different answers.
- Discuss how to check which answer is correct. Draw on the methods and strategies that children wrote down. Ask questions such as:
  - *How did you start?*
  - *What did you need to know?*
  - *Why did you do it this way?*
  - *Can you show me this using a number line?*
  - *Who did it differently?*
  - *What have we missed?*
  - *How many squares to the end of the row?*
  - *Is there a quicker way of doing this?*
  - *Would that work for the yellow and red counters?*
- Children return to their pairs and work out how many squares blue needs to move to catch up with yellow.

★ Snowballing
- Pairs talk to each other about the relative positions of the counters on the board, e.g. *"Yellow is above and to the right of blue"*. They come up with as many statements as possible.
- At a given signal, they join another pair. Pairs take it in turns to share their statements.

AfL Can children describe where objects are on a game board?
Can children find a difference by counting on?

⚠ Challenge
Children choose a ladder. *How many squares does it let you miss out? Try other ladders.*

KEY VOCABULARY
count on, places, squares, row, column, ten, hundred, right, left, above, below, up, down

Name _____ Date _____

FUN WITH POSITION

You need an old postcard or birthday card.

★ Cut the card into 7 or more interesting shapes.

★ Shuffle the shapes.

★ Put the card back together.

Write or tell someone how to do it.

Use position words like **next to**, **above**, **below**, **under**.

GETTING THERE

Introduction
- Load up the *Mind's Eye* CD-ROM. Ask children for an initial response to what they see.
- Ask children what is happening in the photograph. Establish that these children are leaving school at the end of the day. Discuss how children get to school and go home.

Discussion
- Invite children to describe what they can see. Ask questions such as:
  - *How might these children get to school?*
  - *Why do you think that?*
  - *Which is the quickest way for you to get to school?*
  - *Is that always the case?*
  - *What can slow you down?*

© Catherine Yeulet/iStockphoto

Content focus

Block D, Unit 3 – use vocabulary related to time; talk about days of the week and months of the year

ACTIVITIES

★ Rainbowing
- Say: *Josh and Dan are friends. They leave for school in the morning at the same time. Dan gets there first. How can that be?*
- In groups of three, children talk about this and give their reasons. They take turns to speak. Encourage them to discuss their reasons with each other and to listen carefully.
- After a few minutes, allocate group members the colour blue, yellow or red. Children form new single-colour groups.
- Children in single-colour groups take turns to tell each other the explanations that their original groups found. *How many different reasons can you think of?*
- Finally, hold a whole-class discussion about children's ideas. Encourage children to find a way to classify their reasons, e.g. how they travel, where they live, what they do on the way.

★ Think, pair, share
- Ask children to think about their favourite school day.
- After some individual thinking time, they join with a partner. Ask them to take turns to talk about their favourite school day and to give their reasons. They focus on lessons or events that they enjoy.
- Hold a whole-class discussion about children's ideas. Ask questions about times and days such as:
  - *Have you all chosen the same day?*
  - *Why not?*
  - *Why did you choose that day?*
  - *What time does that happen?*
  - *Is that before or after lunchtime?*
  - *What do we do after lunch on Friday?*
  - *What happens every day at 10 o'clock?*

> **AfL** Can children use vocabulary related to time? Can children read time to the nearest half-hour?

❗ Challenge
Give children this problem. *It is seven o'clock. Pia wants to watch a film that is two hours long. She has to go to bed at 8.30. Does she have time to watch the film? Explain your thinking.*

KEY VOCABULARY
time, clock, morning, afternoon, evening, hour, night, day, week, month, year, days of the week

Name _____   Date _____

GETTING THERE

Ask 10 people what time they go to bed.
Make a list of their answers.

Times

How many people go to bed before you?

How many people go to bed after you?

How many people go to bed at the same time as you?

FAIRGROUND RIDE

Introduction
- Load up the *Mind's Eye* CD-ROM. Ask children for an initial response to what they see.
- In Roman times, fairs were holidays. The largest fair in the world took place in India in 2001 when 60 million people gathered at the Kumbh Mela.
- Ask children about trips they have made to the fair or a theme park. Funfairs have many rides for children. *What do you like to do at a fair?* Talk about merry-go-rounds, teacup rides, bumper cars, etc.

Discussion
- Invite children to describe what they can see.
- Ask questions such as:
  - What ride is this?
  - What shape is a roundabout?
  - How much do you think this ride costs?
  - If the ride costs 25p, what coins could you pay with?
  - What if you had three 10ps? How much change would you get?
  - How could you pay for a ride that costs 20p?
  - Is there another way?
  - How could you do that with fewer coins?

© iStockphoto

Content focus
Block D, Unit 3 – solve mathematical problems or puzzles; find totals, give change and work out which coins to pay with

ACTIVITIES

★ Rainbowing
- Children will need coins.
- Give groups of three children this problem to work on. *Harry had a ride at the fair. It cost less than 20p. Harry paid with 3 coins. How much did he pay?*
- Rainbow groups work out how to pay an amount less than 20p with three coins. They find all the ways they can. All children record their solutions so that they can share them with their single-colour groups.
- Allocate group members the colour blue, yellow or red. Children form new single-colour groups.
- Children in single-colour groups share their solutions and develop new ones.
- Finally, hold a whole-class discussion about children's solutions. Single-colour groups take turns to present a solution. The rest of the class checks for correct answers and to see if they had found that answer themselves.

★ Snowballing
- In pairs, children play Target Number. The first player writes 1, 2 or 3. The second player adds 1, 2 or 3 to the number. Take turns adding 1, 2 or 3. The winner is the player who gets 18.
- After pairs have played this game a few times, they talk about how they play the game. They explain their strategies to each other.
- Pairs join to make fours. Pairs play the game against each other. Children talk to each other and agree what to do before they add their next number.

AfL Do children relate addition to counting on? Do children recognise that addition can be done in any order? Can children use practical and informal written methods to support the addition of a one-digit number to another one-digit or two-digit number?

⚠ Challenge
Ask children to imagine that the target is 14 and it is their turn to start. *Can you win? Explain.*

KEY VOCABULARY
money, coin, pence, penny, pay, change, price, spend, not enough, add on, more, too much

FAIRGROUND RIDE

This ride costs 25p.

Show all the ways you could pay.

ALLSORTS

Introduction
- Load up the *Mind's Eye* CD-ROM. Ask children for an initial response to what they see.
- Explain that there is a story that liquorice allsorts were invented by accident. Just over a hundred years ago, Charlie Thompson, a salesperson, is supposed to have dropped a tray of mixed sweets that he was showing someone. This meant that all the sweets got mixed up. He scrambled to re-arrange them and the person he was talking to really liked the new-look sweets. So the company began to make the allsorts and they became very popular.

Discussion
- Discuss the allsorts shown in the photograph. Encourage children to describe what they see.
- Ask related questions such as:
  – How many different sorts are there here?
  – Which of these shapes will roll?
  – Can you think of some names to give the different types of sweets?
  – How could we sort them out?
  – How could we sort the sweets into two sets? Could we do that a different way?
  – How could we sort the sweets into three sets?

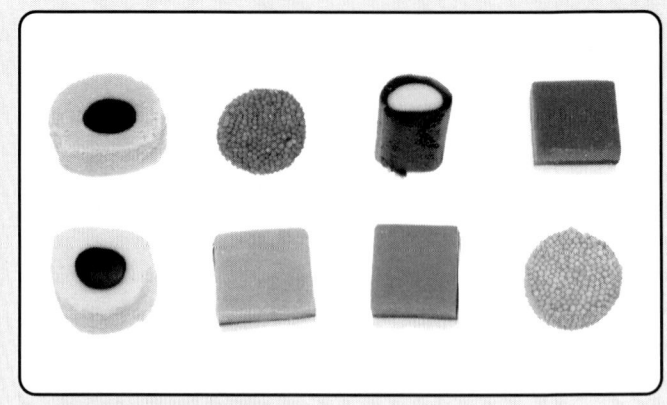

© Enjoylife25/Dreamstime.com

  – Can you describe the position of the orange allsort?
  – How can we split the set into two equal halves? Is there a different way?
  – Can you count them in twos? What would the next number be?

Content focus
Block E, Unit 1 – describe and solve a puzzle or problem

ACTIVITIES

⭐ Envoy
- Invite each home group to explore the number of ways that they could choose two sweets from the picture.
- Ask groups to discuss how they might tackle this investigation before they start. Encourage them to keep track of their ideas on paper or to use practical equipment such as cubes or 3-D shapes.
- When each group has found a few possibilities, choose group envoys. The envoy moves to another group and listens to their ideas. The envoy then returns to their home group and reports what they have learned.
- Children should decide how to record their solutions. Encourage them to explain their findings in the context of the original problem.

⭐ Think, pair, share
- Children will need whiteboards or paper and pens.
- Ask children to imagine that the green and orange square sweets have changed places. After visualising this, they record the new arrangement. Compare solutions.
- Ask: *How many moves would it take to rearrange the sweets so that all the square sweets are together and all the sweets with sprinkles are together? Swapping places counts as one move.*
- Clarify the meaning of 'together' as next to one another. Invite children to clarify the rules. For example, swapping the orange sweet with the black and white one will put the orange square sweet next to the brown one.
- Children work on this problem individually before joining a partner to develop a joint solution.
- Pairs share their ideas with the class. Encourage them to explain their methods using drawings.

AfL Can children show and explain how they solved a problem using drawings or objects?
Can children visualise the position of the sweets when they have changed places?

❗ Challenge
Give children this problem. *If each liquorice allsort costs 2p, how much would they cost altogether? What if they cost 5p each?*

KEY VOCABULARY
best way, another way, different way, sort, group, set, same, different, together, arrange

ALLSORTS

Play with a friend.

Make a pattern like this with cubes.

red	blue	red
blue	red	blue
red	blue	red

★ Close your eyes.
★ Your friend takes away a cube.
★ Open your eyes. Guess the missing colour.

Explain how you know.

Take turns.

SHELLS

Introduction
- Load up the *Mind's Eye* CD-ROM. Ask children for an initial response to what they see.
- Explain that a sea shell has been made by a sea creature that does not need it any more. It is a hard outer layer that keeps the soft creature inside safe. Sea shells are most often found on beaches, washed up by the tide. Some beaches have more shells than others. Shells have been used for money in some parts of the world. A large shell called a conch can be blown through to make a loud noise. People who like making things will often use shells to decorate things like picture frames and boxes to make them look pretty.

Discussion
- Ask children what they notice about the way the sets of shells are arranged. Remind children about doubling.
- Ask questions such as:
  - *How many are there?*
  - *How many would there be if there was another set exactly the same?*
  - *Do we need to add or take away?*
  - *Tell me how to write that.*

© Jenny Penfold

Content focus
Block E, Unit 1 – find doubles of numbers; use the vocabulary of halves in context

ACTIVITIES

★ Snowballing
- Children will need whiteboards or paper and pens, plus counters or small cubes.
- Children start in pairs. They choose some shells from the picture and work out together how many they would have if they had double that number. If they are struggling, encourage them to make two identical sets using counters and add them.
- Children join another pair and work together until they have doubled all the sets of shells.

★ Think, pair, share
- Remind children that they can find half of a set of objects as well as of shapes. Ask them to look at the picture.
- *Can you find half of all these sets of shells?* Working individually, children can do this mentally, using counters or using jottings.
- Children join with a partner and compare their answers. Encourage them to find a way to check their answers.
- Hold a whole-class discussion to share ideas. Ask questions such as:
  - *Which shells can you find half of?*
  - *What do you notice about the sets that you can't halve?*
  - *What if there was one more shell in this set?*
  - *How did you get that answer?*
  - *Can you draw that on the board?*

> **AfL** Do children understand that double 3 is 6 because 3 + 3 = 6?
> Can children recall or work out doubles of numbers to 5 + 5?

⚠ Challenge
What if you doubled all the shells in the picture? Would there be enough for everyone in the class to have one? Explain.

KEY VOCABULARY
double, make, sum, total, altogether, pattern, answer

SHELLS

Draw on each set of shells to show half.

Do it 4 different ways.

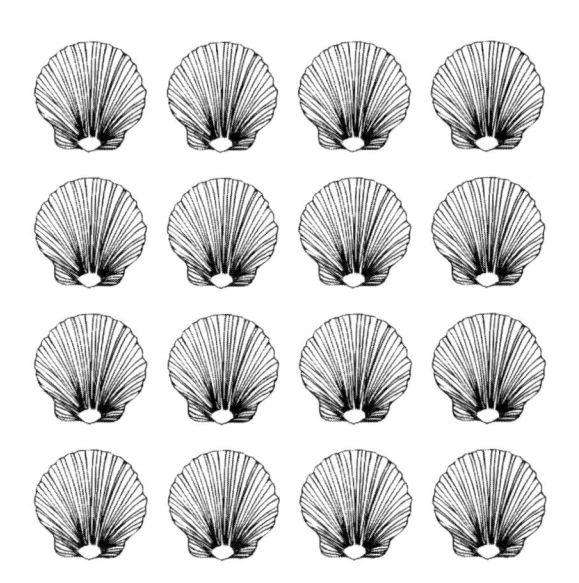

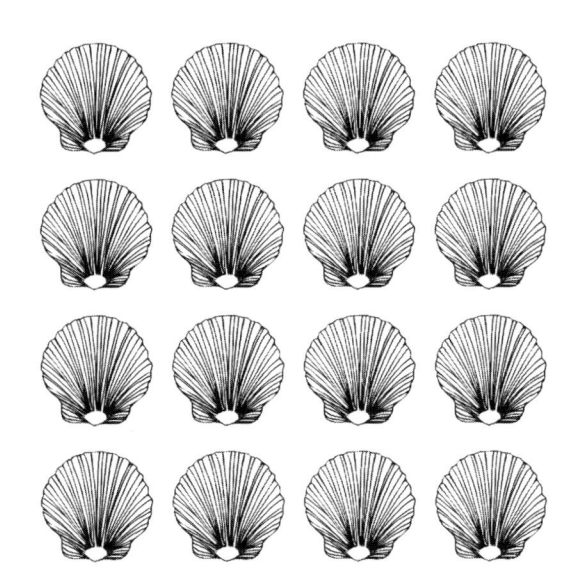

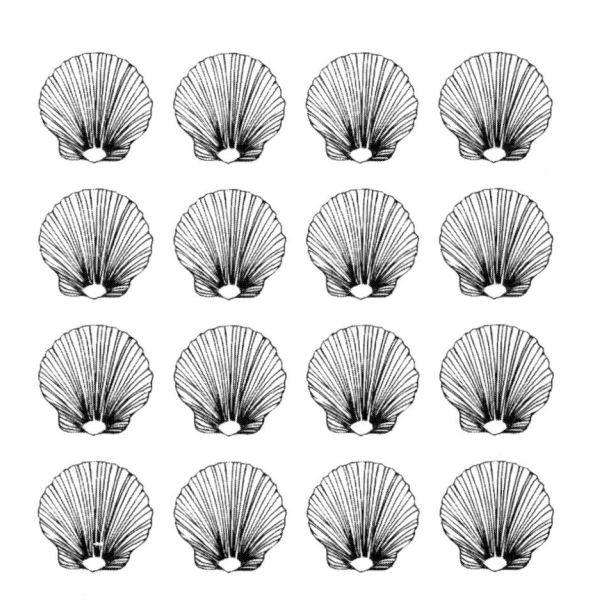

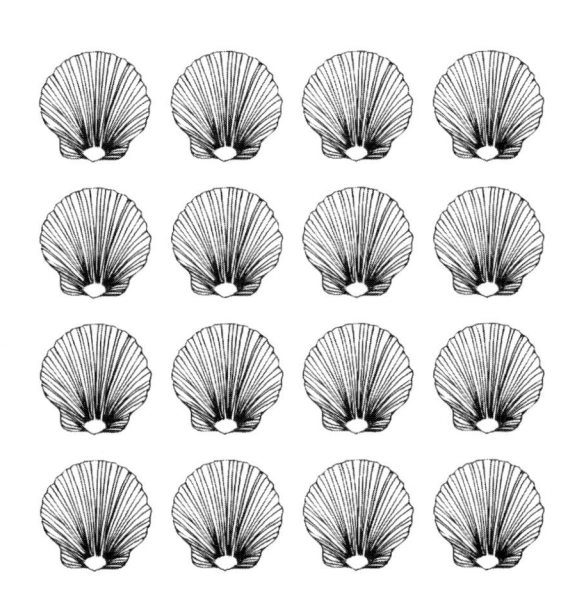

STARFISH

Introduction

- Load up the *Mind's Eye* CD-ROM. Ask children for an initial response to what they see.
- Explain that starfish can be found in rock pools and on beaches. Most are orange. They always have five arms. If they lose an arm they can grow one back. They have rows of feet under their arms and they walk slowly along the sea bed. Their mouth is also under their body. Starfish can push their stomachs out through their mouths. They do this when they are trying to eat something that is too big to swallow.

Discussion

- Ask children to describe what they can see in detail and to share all that they know about starfish with a partner.
- Ask questions such as:
  - *What shape is this?*
  - *How many arms would two starfish have altogether? How did you work that out? Did you count the arms on the first starfish or did you start from five? Why is it a good idea to start from five to answer this question?*

© Carmen Martínez Banús/iStockphoto

Content focus

Block E, Unit 2 – solve problems involving counting, adding, subtracting, doubling or halving in the context of numbers

ACTIVITIES

⭐ Home group

- Children will need strips of paper.
- Give each home group of no more than six children this problem on a piece of paper. A child reads it out to their group:
  - *Mia started at 0 and counted in fives.*
  - *She wrote all the numbers down.*
  - *The middle number was 15.*
  - *What was the biggest number Mia wrote?*
- The group discusses how to solve the problem.
- Children then work in pairs to answer the question. They write their number sequence on their strip of paper.
- When they have all finished, pairs take turns to read out their number sequences and say the middle number. They then place their paper strip on the table until all the pairs have shared their answers.
- The group comes to a joint agreement about the correct answer by comparing the strips of paper.

⭐ Think, pair, share

- Say: *If you write all the numbers from 1 to 50, will you write more ones or more fives?* [The answer is ones.]
- Give children a few minutes to work on this problem individually.
- Children join with a partner to discuss the question and work out a joint solution. They should try to work out the answer without writing down all the numbers from 1 to 50.
- Discuss pairs' ideas with the whole class or group. Ask questions such as:
  - *How did you work it out?*
  - *What did you know before you started?*
  - *Why did you decide to do it this way?*
  - *If you were doing this problem again, how would you do it differently?*
  - *How could we change the question?*

AfL Can children solve problems involving counting in steps of one, two, five or ten?

❗ Challenge

Ask children to count in twos, fives and tens from different numbers, e.g. 3, 5 and 7.

KEY VOCABULARY

middle, count in fives, step, one more, five more

Name _____ Date _____

STARFISH

★ 6 starfish. How many arms?

★ A plastic starfish costs 5p. How many can you buy for 30p?

★ 7 pairs of socks. How many socks altogether?

★ 10 stickers in a box. How many stickers altogether?

★ 10 children. How many eyes altogether?

FEEDING TIME

Introduction
- Load up the *Mind's Eye* CD-ROM. Ask children for an initial response to what they see.
- Explain that the robin is often called the UK's favourite bird. You can tell it by its bright red breast. Males and females look the same. Robins sing nearly all year round and they are very pretty to look at. At night they will sing next to street lights. Robins defend their territory and will drive away strange birds. Robins eat worms, seeds, fruits and insects. This robin is bringing worms to baby birds in the nest. Robins can build nests in funny places like old kettles or plant pots. The baby birds hatch from about two weeks.

Discussion
- Ask children to describe what they can see. Ask related questions such as:
  - *Have you ever seen a bird's nest? Where?*
  - *How many baby birds can you see?*
  - *Are there enough worms for every chick to have one?*

© Jeff Chiasson/iStockphoto

Content focus
Block E, Unit 2 – solve practical problems that involve combining groups of 2, 5 or 10, or sharing into equal groups

ACTIVITIES

★ Think, pair, share
- Children will need whiteboards or paper and pens.
- Say: *A bird has four chicks in the nest. She brings two worms for every chick to eat. How many worms does she bring?*
- Children work on the problem individually for a few minutes.
- They then join a partner to discuss how they could find the answer. They work on their solution together, recording their method. Encourage them to use number sentences or drawings.
- When children have completed the task, work with the whole class. Invite children to talk about their method and show their working.
- Drawing on methods and strategies, ask questions such as:
  - *Did you add or subtract?*
  - *Why did you do it this way?*
  - *What did you need to know?*
  - *Did anyone do it differently? Why?*
  - *How could we write that as a number sentence?*
  - *What if there are five chicks/six chicks?*

★ Snowballing
- Children will need A4 or larger paper.
- Say: *A bird finds ten worms. She can only carry one worm at a time. Find a way to make sure that her five chicks get the same number of worms.*
- Children join with a partner to find a way to show on paper how all the chicks get fed.
- At a given signal, children join another pair. Pairs compare their work and check that all the chicks get the same number of worms. They listen carefully to the way that the other pair has tackled the problem. *How did you share out the worms?*

AfL Can children show how they solved a problem, using drawings or objects to help?
Can children share into equal groups and say how many in each group?

❗ Challenge
Children work out the secret number. *It is greater than 6 + 7. It is less than 9 + 9. You say it when you count in twos. It is not 8 + 8.*

KEY VOCABULARY
equal, groups, twos, share, greater than, less than

Name _____ Date _____

FEEDING TIME

Mother bird gave 2 worms to each chick.

How many worms were not eaten?

Show how you know.

COUNTING COINS

Introduction
- Load up the *Mind's Eye* CD-ROM. Ask children for an initial response to what they see.
- Ask children to tell you about the coins they have learned about so far.

Discussion
- Discuss the coins shown, asking questions such as:
  - *How much money is here?*
  - *How much more is needed to make 30p?*
  - *How many 2p sweets could you buy with this money?*
  - *If this person dropped 10p just before the photo was taken, how much money did they start off with?*
  - *Can you say these coins in order, starting with the one that is worth least?*
  - *What if this person has the same amount in the other hand?*
  - *Could you make the same amount with different coins?*

© Rising Stars UK Ltd.

Content focus
Block E, Unit 3 – describe patterns and relationships involving numbers

ACTIVITIES

★ Think, pair, share
- Say: *Sam has only 10p, 5p and 2p coins. He pays for a comic costing 50p using exactly six of his coins. Which coins did he use?*
- After initial individual thinking time, children work out the solution with a partner and share these with the class.

★ Envoy
- Children will need coins and a large piece of paper.
- Ask groups of three to explore the numbers of ways they can make 10p, 20p, 30p and so on.
- Groups should discuss how to tackle this investigation before getting started. Encourage them to think about how to share out the work.
- Choose an envoy from each group to move to a different group and listen to their ideas. The envoy then returns to their own group and reports on what they have learned.
- Children decide how to present their work and make a poster to show their results. Each group joins with another. Groups take turns to explain what they have found out to each other.

★ Snowballing
- Children need whiteboards or paper and pens, plus a number of 10p and 5p coins.
- Ask children to work in pairs. They put down a 10p, then a 5p next to it, then a 10p and continue until they have put down ten coins.
- Children talk to each other about the pattern they have made. They then make up three questions to ask another pair, and work out the answers.
- At a given signal, pairs join to make fours. Pairs take it in turns to ask each other one of their questions.

AfL Can children make amounts to 20p and beyond with coins?

❗ Challenge
Children fill in the blanks with numbers. The story must make sense.
Max had _____ p. He bought a pencil for _____ p. He has _____ p left.

KEY VOCABULARY
money, coin, add on, more, pay, change, pattern

COUNTING COINS

Sam has 2 coins.

Together they make less than 50p and more than 10p.

What coins could they be?

DUCKS

Introduction
- Load up the *Mind's Eye* CD-ROM. Ask children for an initial response to what they see.
- Ask children to tell you everything they know about ducks.
- Establish that the picture shows a type of duck called a mallard. Mallards are the most familiar ducks in Britain. They live in all sorts of different places where there is water. They spend most of their time in the water. Like all ducks, mallards have webbed feet that help them move quickly in the water. Ducks waddle when they walk because their two legs are towards the back of their bodies.

Discussion
- Invite children to describe what they can see.
- Ask questions such as:
  - *How many eggs can you see?*
  - *How are they arranged?*
  - *If half the eggs hatch out to be male, how many will be female?*
  - *If one duckling is female, how many will be male?*
  - *Could we count these eggs in twos?*

Content focus
Block E, Unit 3 – solve practical problems that involve combining groups of 2, 5 or 10, or sharing into equal groups

© Sahua/Dreamstime.com

ACTIVITIES

★ Think, pair, share
- Give children this problem to work on individually at first. *When Daphne Duck counts her eggs in twos, she has one left over. When she counts them in fives, she has none left over. How many eggs does she have?*
- At a given signal, they join a partner. Children explain their thinking so far and decide on any apparatus they need to help them with the problem, e.g. number lines or counters.
- Children collaborate to solve the problem. Encourage them to think about whether they could divide up the work in some way.
- The class meets up to compare their answers and methods. They check solutions using a different method.

AfL Can children solve a problem involving counting using apparatus or a diagram?

⚠ Challenge
Choose some different numbers, e.g. 3, 4. *When the duck counts her eggs in threes, does she have any left over? What if she counts them in fours?*

KEY VOCABULARY
count, twos, fives, tens, equal, left over

Name _____   Date _____

DUCKS

How many eyes and legs do 2 ducks have altogether?

Draw different numbers of ducks. Make up questions about them.

OVERVIEW OF *MIND'S EYE TALK FOR MATHS* BOOK 1

Mind's Eye images	Framework ref.	Mathematical content focus	Classroom techniques for group discussion									
			Envoy	Home group	Hot seating	Listening triangles	Rainbowing	Snowballing	Talk partners	Think, pair, share	Whole class
Snowmen	A1	Solve problems involving counting						★		★	
Count away	A1	Solve problems involving counting						★		★	
In my home	A2	Compare and order numbers		★		★					
Making numbers	A2	Problems involving addition and subtraction						★		★	
Car numbers	A3	Use knowledge of place value to position numbers to 20 and beyond on a number track and number line; know addition and subtraction facts to at least 10						★		★	
Animal sums	A3	Solve problems involving counting and adding numbers						★	★		
Triangles and squares	B1	Visualise and name 2-D shapes, describing their features							★	★	
Dominoes	B1	Early addition and subtraction using related language and symbols				★		★			
Money box	B2	Problems involving money					★	★			
Would you rather?	B2	Problems involving money					★	★			
Patterns	B2	Describe simple patterns and relationships						★		★	
Airbrick patterns	B3	Visualise and name common 2-D shapes and 3-D solids, describing their features; use them to make patterns, pictures and models		★				★			
Cupcakes	B3	Solve problems involving adding and subtracting; count on in steps of 3 or 4 from zero, or from any small number	★					★			
Shapes and patterns	B3	Visualise and name common 2-D shapes; use them to make patterns, pictures and models		★					★		
Sorting	C1	Sort information and communicate findings						★	★		
A bit longer or shorter	C1	Measure and compare lengths					★	★			
Same and different	C2	Sort information according to a given criterion							★	★	
Ice-cream	C3	Answer a question by recording information in lists and tables; present outcomes using practical resources, pictures, block graphs or pictograms		★							★
Positions	D1	Visualise and use everyday language to describe the position of objects				★					★
How to pay	D1	Solve problems involving counting, adding, subtracting in the context of money							★	★	
Times	D2	Use vocabulary related to time; order events		★				★			
Fun with position	D2	Reasoning about position, direction and movement; relate addition to counting on						★		★	
Getting there	D3	Use vocabulary related to time; talk about days of the week and months of the year					★			★	
Fairground ride	D3	Solve mathematical problems or puzzles; find totals, give change, and work out which coins to pay with					★	★			
Allsorts	E1	Describe and solve a puzzle or problem	★							★	
Shells	E1	Find doubles of numbers; use the vocabulary of halves in context						★		★	
Starfish	E2	Solve problems involving counting, adding, subtracting, doubling or halving in the context of numbers		★						★	
Feeding time	E2	Solve practical problems that involve combining groups of 2, 5 or 10, or sharing into equal groups						★		★	
Counting coins	E3	Describe patterns and relationships involving numbers	★					★			
Ducks	E3	Solve practical problems that involve combining groups of 2, 5 or 10, or sharing into equal groups								★	